AUSTIN ROVER
MAESTRO AND
MONTEGO

SAM SKELTON

AMBERLEY

First published 2023

Amberley Publishing
The Hill, Stroud,
Gloucestershire, GL5 4EP

www.amberley-books.com

ISBN: 978 1 3981 0215 6 (print)
ISBN: 978 1 3981 0216 3 (ebook)

British Library Cataloguing in Publication Data.
A catalogue record for this book is available from the British Library.

Typeset in 10pt on 13pt Celeste.
Typesetting by SJmagic DESIGN SERVICES, India.
Printed in the UK.

CONTENTS

INTRODUCTION

History perhaps doesn't look back so fondly on the Austin Maestro – nor upon its sister, the Montego – as it should. To many, these cars are derided as the perfect example of the failing of British industry: undesirable and bland family cars at best, and atrocities at worst. But they're also among the most relatable old cars on the road; everybody knew someone who had a Maestro or a Montego, and regardless of what we may have felt about them there is an undeniable nostalgia that comes with age when looking back at the cars that once surrounded us.

The fact that it has taken almost forty years for a book to be written documenting these cars says a lot about wider perception of these models over the years, but hopefully the story it contains will make you think twice before dismissing what were in fact competent cars in a market that placed too much emphasis on brand image. Sold as an Austin, an MG, a Vanden Plas and – in its latter years – with no clear brand identification at all, the humble Maestro and Montego may have sold 1.2 million combined against the Ford Sierra's 3.5 million, but their long production run and hardy mechanicals meant that many were still in service over a decade after production ended in 1994.

While many credit the Maestro and Montego with effectively killing off British Leyland as a major player in the fleet sector, the fact remains that without the budget to develop an effective car by the end of the 1970s BL was always going to have lost ground, and the market climate into which they were launched was not the fault of the products themselves. Indeed, both matured into excellent, reliable transport for those unburdened by image worries.

During the course of this book, we will discover that they had a difficult job in consolidating and replacing myriad models which went before, that design delays didn't help, but that they ultimately became hardy and long-lasting beasts of burden for owners who simply wouldn't contemplate anything else. We will take a look at the development of both models, the way they evolved through production, and focus on some of the more exciting halo models at the top of the ranges – overlooked cars in an image conscious market. We will consider some of the alternative uses that they were put to by external coachbuilders, and we will examine what became of them once Britain had had its fill. Should you be tempted into ownership by the end of the book, there's even a handy buying guide.

I hope you enjoy reading this book as much as I have enjoyed researching and writing it, and as much as I have enjoyed my own experience of life within the Maestro and Montego fold. I have owned multiple Montegos and spent several years on the club committee before the majority of people began to recognise these cars as the collectibles that they truly are. As time passes and their classic status becomes ever more assured, it brings me great pleasure to see new enthusiasts enter the fold. Hopefully, this book will help to attract even more.

It would be remiss of me not to thank former Maestro and Montego Club Archivist Simon Heap for his contributions, primarily from his image and brochure archive but also in proofreading this book. I also owe a debt to Keith Adams, as creator of www. aronline.co.uk – a fantastic web resource and one without which research would have been infinitely more difficult.

Maestros and Montegos today enjoy an ardent following.

1

BRITISH LEYLAND'S MID-RANGE IN THE 1970S

To understand the Maestro and Montego ranges and where they sat in the Leyland hierarchy, it's best to look back to the previous decade, and the somewhat convoluted and confused middle ground of the existing British Leyland range. Where rivals such as Ford could offer a clear and coherent range of models with clear delineation, the formation of British Leyland at the end of the 1960s had led to misunderstanding among marques and no sense of direction. Models were launched without key features for fear of internal competition, and it was evident that the range would need some measure of rationalisation. A clear brand strategy would be vital moving forward, given that many factories and dealers still identified as Austin or Morris rather than as Leyland. This didn't help quell the sense of internal rivalry created by the wide choice of models.

Marina   twice the car for your money.

The Morris Marina was outdated by the late 1970s.

Above: The oft-derided Austin Allegro would need replacing too.

Below: The Maxi sat uncomfortably within the BL range.

Five years before the launch of the Maestro and during the development of that car, British Leyland offered a choice of three mainstream models under three brands at the lower end of the middle market – the Morris Marina, the Austin Allegro and the Maxi, shorn by this time of its Austin branding. British Leyland had fiercely guarded the market position of the Maxi by ensuring that neither the Allegro nor the larger Princess were to be made available as hatchbacks, but it was observed by many in the motoring press that the Marina and the Allegro were effectively competing with each other. This was correct – to a degree. The Marina had been launched as a fleet market chaser to target the Cortina and Escort, given that the complex and compact ADO16 was losing ground to Dagenham. The Allegro would eventually replace the ADO16 range in full with a new, advanced, compact saloon. While the two cars were marketed very differently, there is no denying that they appealed to the same audiences and profit could be maximised by removing this internal competition. The Marina and Allegro estates were both indirectly in competition with Maxi, too, but British Leyland would fiercely defend what felt like an unnecessary model. In 1980, the Marina would be refined into the Ital – effectively a heavy facelift, hoped to be enough to tide the car over until its replacement was launched – but it was on borrowed time from day one.

Marina estate was a dependable if dated load lugger.

Austin Allegro 2
1300 AND 1500 ESTATE

Allegro estate was practical but undesirable.

Further up the range, the top end of the Cortina market and the lower end of the Granada market were spanned by the Leyland Princess; introduced in 1975 under three separate marques which would be combined just nine months later. In 1.8-litre guise this was just as important to the upper end of the fleet segment as the upmarket models from the Marina line. The Princess would be replaced by the Austin Ambassador – which would finally give it the hatchback it had long needed – but long term, like the Ital, the Ambassador itself would need replacing.

Technically the Maestro was touted as a replacement for the Allegro, which had offered a choice of two- or four-door saloon bodies plus a three-door estate. However, in concept it proved far nearer to the Maxi given that it was to be offered solely as a five-door hatchback in a bid to retain customers both from the popular four-door Allegro and from the Maxi itself. The Marina, of course, was primarily available in saloon and estate forms – the Coupe was a budget offering, but one that was unnecessary given that the new range would incorporate the budget Maestro for those not in need of a large four-door saloon.

It was the Ital that the Montego was planned primarily to replace – taking the existing Maestro development, elongating the wheelbase and redesigning just enough of the body to justify its positioning in a different market class. Reusing the same door skins wasn't new for the industry, nor especially for BL. The outgoing Maxi used doors that had been seen before on the Austin 1800 and Austin 3-litre of the 1960s. As time passed and the Princess saloon began to look dated, BL felt that long term it would be replaced by

9

THE 18-22 SERIES. The car that's got it all together.

Left: The larger 18-22 series would evolve into the Princess.

Below: The Princess's market share would be taken by Montego and low-end Rovers.

Above: Like the Marina, the Princess received a late facelift – the Ambassador gained a hatchback.

Below: The Ital was the car Montego had to replace.

upmarket Montegos and low-spec Rovers to better mirror the market positioning of its rivals. The Princess had also been denied a hatchback in order to maintain Maxi sales, so upmarket Montego estates might even broaden the range's appeal. The short-term fix of introducing the Austin Ambassador until the Montego was production ready demonstrated that there was a market for an opening tailgate at this level of the marketplace, whether hatchback or estate was the chosen configuration.

This range would effectively continue the rationalisation process instigated by the 1975 Ryder Report, which concluded that the middle of British Leyland's range was confusing and ultimately costing the company profit. In less than ten years, the Austin brand would not only have supplanted Wolseley but also Morris and Vanden Plas, leading to a clearer choice for the consumer between clearly defined models unified under a single brand. Moreover, the mid-market range would condense from an initial choice of four separate model offerings to just two – themselves based around the same fundamental package. Financially, for a company with limited resources, the plan made sense. By eliminating any sense of internal competition, it looked to be a move which would also maximise profit.

2

DEVELOPMENT OF THE MAESTRO

The Marina's sensibility and simplicity was what Leyland needed moving forward, and it's important to note that of the three the Marina was the strongest seller, with production close to equalling the joint total of the two mid-range Austins. As early as 1975, Spen King and Gordon Bashford were working on the project which would later become LC10, but it only became a production reality after the appointment of Michael Edwardes to BL in November 1977. Having focused initially upon the Metro, he then turned his attention and BL funding to the mid-market. This was where the range was weakest. BL may have had Allegro, Marina, Maxi and Dolomite but all were ageing designs and a replacement had to be the highest priority. The King and Bashford proposal followed the Marina in terms of its design simplicity, but updated it for the 1980s – transverse engine, front-wheel drive, end on gearbox, and no Hydragas – effectively a straight copy of the Volkswagen Golf. The culling of the proposed new small Triumph range meant that all mid-range attention was now focused on the LC10 programme – the cars which would become Maestro and Montego. Edwardes cancelled a number of projects, including the Rover SD1 estate, Princess estate and Triumph Lynx, in order to ensure funding could be channelled toward these new models.

Despite the UK market's fondness for saloons, BL made the decision to develop the smaller, hatchback model ahead of the saloon. The rationale was simple: the export markets BL was so keen to court were shifting toward the hatchback, and this was planned to be the volume seller outside Britain. The plan was to release the saloon within a year of the hatchback model.

The engines to be used were easily chosen. The smaller size would be catered for by the A-series range, but the larger engine size was more controversial. Plans to use the 1.7-litre O-series were abandoned partly because of space considerations, but also because the market demanded a 1.6. Fortunately, the E-series tooling still existed, and a 1,598cc development of that engine was implemented as an interim solution while the new S-series was developed. This interim engine, the R-series, would be used only in the first fifteen months of Maestro production, and never in the later Montego. Gearboxes would be drawn from the Volkswagen Group, buying them in cost profit but saving the cost of designing an all new unit.

The A-series was a logical choice for the new car.

Above: Harris Mann proposal was neat, but BL preferred the Ian Beech proposal.

Below: Early prototypes featured Allegro-style headlamps and metal bumpers.

Two designs had been proposed: one by Harris Mann, and the other by Ian Beech working under David Bache. The latter was the design that was chosen, despite the former being an arguably more modern shape. But it became evident that a design developed in 1976 would be outdated even by launch in 1983. Managing Director Harold Musgrove was astounded by the design of the car when first presented with it in 1982, stating that a car should remind him of his girlfriend, while this one reminded him of his grandmother. A subsequent design disagreement would lead to his dismissal of David Bache and the employment of Roy Axe in his place, but with under a year to go until production began there was little that could be done to change the Maestro's shape.

Fortunately, BL had planned two industry firsts for the Maestro to bring the design more up to date. First was the use of painted plastic bumpers – not new in and of itself but revolutionary for the mass market. Unlike the Citroën BX and subsequent facelifted CX, these were painted with the car rather than moulded in colour. The wings were modified to take the new bumpers, fitted to all but the base model, which would continue to wear the black metal units originally designed. Second was the use of an electronic dashboard. BL was actually beaten to market by one week by Renault, but its digital dashboard was a more advanced unit than the French design. It used solid state technology combined with an on-board trip computer and voice synthesiser, voiced by New Zealand actor Nicolette MacKenzie. Thirty-two words were recorded in a total of fifteen languages, warning of basic issues such as unfastened seatbelts or low oil pressure. The system was fitted as standard to the Vanden Plas and MG models and listed as an option for HLS, but would be made optional on MG models only for 1985 and finally deleted for 1986.

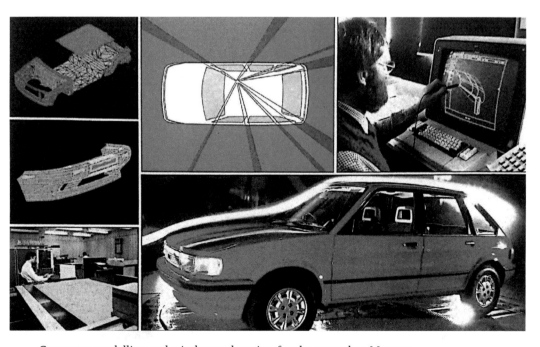

Computer modelling and wind tunnel testing for the up-to-date Maestro.

Above: Most Maestros came with these plastic bumpers.

Left: The LCD dash display was reserved for upmarket models.

Below: The initial range.

THE MIRACLE MAESTRO
DRIVING IS BELIEVING

Production began in November 1982, in readiness for the car's 1 March 1983 launch. The range at launch comprised seven models: 1.3, 1.3L, 1.6L, 1.3HLE, 1.6HLS, 1.6 Vanden Plas and MG 1600. The HLE employed special long gearing and an econometer to boost parsimony, and would continue to 1986. There would briefly be an economy-focused LE based on the L by way of replacement.

While the dealers, press and public liked the Maestro at first, and while by 2 March Austin Rover was boasting of £50 million in fleet orders for the new car, sales ultimately were not as strong as the company had hoped. Key to this was its positioning in the fleet sector, and the considerable discounts rivals Ford were able to offer to fleet buyers. Austin Rover simply couldn't compete on price, and the issue was compounded when within the first month 7,000 workers at the Cowley factory walked out on strike for a full four

Above: Economy-focused HLE had aerodynamic aids.

Right: HLEs also received an econometer.

weeks. The initial momentum was lost, and by then reports were creeping into the press of unreliability – hot starting issues with the MG and erratic voice synthesisers were just the tip of the iceberg. Austin Rover's marketing strategy didn't help either; adverts pushed the company rather than its products, and while people were begged to 'Move Over to Austin Rover' and told by Noel Edmonds that the company offered 'Driving At Its Best', the new car wasn't highlighted as strongly as it should have been. Confused marketing also saw the company attempt to pitch the Maestro as a Sierra competitor in the months leading up to the Montego launch, leaving buyers bewildered as to what the car really was.

Rumours of a Ford takeover during 1985 didn't help the Maestro – or its new sister car, the Montego – in terms of sales, with buyers reluctant to buy what may become an obsolete model. When Ford pulled out, sales recovered helped in no small part by the Maestro's new one-piece dashboard sourced from the Montego, but were still sluggish compared to Ford and Vauxhall. The marque was deemed to be the problem, and BL resorted to marketing in a bid to sell the car.

First, it employed Kevin Morley, formerly of Ford, to spearhead a new marketing campaign. The 1.3L and 1.6L were revamped, with duotone paintwork and new maroon inserts, in a bid to market the car as a sportier prospect to a younger audience. This marketing, tied to that of the Montego 1.6L and 2.0Si, was bolstered in June 1987 with a slight facelift and the dropping of the Austin badge from the tailgate. By November of the same year the Austin name had gone completely, replaced on the nose and steering wheel with simple Maestro badging. The facelift of June 1988 would synchronise the specifications with the new Rover range, but by then most of the impetus behind Maestro marketing had gone. New introductions such as the Perkins Prima 65 diesel engine for 1988 and its turbocharged Prima 80 sibling for 1992 would keep Maestro competitive in the budget sector, but the newly named Rover Group's focus by then was on the aspirational R8 200 and 400 series, next to which Maestro seemed antediluvian at best. Arguably the model's last gasp at customer appeal was the Maestro Turbo of 1988, a limited edition model that is covered in greater detail in another chapter.

Above left: The early dashboard was prone to squeaks and rattles.

Above right: Advertising focused upon the company, not its products.

Scant change for the facelift.

3

DEVELOPMENT OF THE MONTEGO

While the gap between the two launches may suggest a different story, the LM10 and LM11 projects were always interlinked and it was always intended that there would be a larger variant derived from the Maestro's underpinnings. British Leyland's mid-sized range was in turmoil; plans to replace the Marina with ADO77 had been axed, as had the Triumph proposal to replace the Dolomite. The Ital was out of date, and while the Triumph Acclaim offered brief respite BL knew it needed to step up and replace the Ital with a new design if it was to retain any hold of the fleet and family car market. And the LM11 was all it had – a saloon derivative based upon the LM10 Maestro. Its wheelbase was set at the original Maestro proposal length – the finished Maestro had a wheelbase 61mm shorter than had been planned initially – and initial proposals centred around the ideal of 'Maestro with a boot' in a similar manner to the subsequent Ford Orion and Vauxhall Belmont.

But this sat at odds with the market position that was needed for the new car to show any sign of success, and it was clear that a restyle using key componentry from the smaller

The first full Montego prototype shows clear signs of the production model.

car would be a more successful approach to take. Roger Tucker's revisions to the front and rear successfully changed the outward appearance of the car, lending it a lower bonnet line, high boot and more of a wedge appearance. When Roy Axe was employed in 1982 as Styling Director, he would apply the finishing touches, reworking the nose, fitting the window trims and revising the rear window area to tighten the design. He had wanted to scrap the lot and redesign the car from scratch, but BL had neither the time nor the money to invest in the Montego. It had to be in production for spring of 1984, and any delay would cost the company money it simply didn't have.

Delays would also potentially impact upon what was looking like a favourable market for Montego. The replacement of Ford's Cortina in 1982 with the bold new Sierra has left fleet buyers nonplussed, and many had jumped ship to Vauxhall's new Mk2 Cavalier with its advanced front-wheel drive layout but conservative body. This trend sat perfectly with the Montego's layout and showed that there would be potential for the new design. In trying to out-discount each other, Ford and Vauxhall had caused confusion for a number of fleet buyers, and the Montego would be the ideal car to plug the gap.

Or it would have been, had the market not failed to see the appeal from day one. Launched on 25 April 1984, the initial range consisted of 1.3- and 1.6-litre base models, a 1.6L, 1.6 and 2.0HL, 2.0HLS, 2.0 Vanden Plas and MG EFi – an effective mid-range, which offered counterparts to almost all Cavalier and Sierra alternatives. Montego may have been a nicer place to be than the Maestro, courtesy of its new interior. It may have been sweeter to drive in 2.0 form courtesy of a new gearbox co-designed with Honda. But a combination

S-series 1.6 meant that the Montego could enjoy a lower bonnet line.

AUSTIN MONTEGO RANGE

Above: The initial Montego range.

Left: The O-series would prove effective in top models.

of strike action and the ongoing price war between Ford and Vauxhall meant that the Montego wasn't seen as an appealing prospect; more expensive than its established rivals, harder to get, and – were the damning long-term test reports by *Autocar* and *Motor* anything to go by – more trying to live with. In addition, Austin Rover's attempt to be at the vanguard of new technology with 365mm TD wheels failed – the rest of the market stuck with imperial wheels and conventional rims, and this peculiarity deterred those seeking sensible transport over fears of tyre availability and price. Far from its projection of 4,000 cars sold per week, by the end of 1984 fewer than 35,000 had been sold; and BL was exploring staff redeployments and layoffs to justify dropping production by a further 10 per cent.

A slight reprieve would follow in the form of the Montego estate. Styled by John Ashford and launched at the 1984 British Motor Show, the awkward rear end of the saloon had been replaced by something neat and well-integrated, with a large boot and optional third row

Above: Montego estate earned itself a Design Council award.

Right: Commodious, it proved popular with families.

of seats making it a credible alternative to the Renault Espace for families who didn't want the appearance of a van. With the seats folded away, there was a flat boot floor with a dip in the rear bumper to facilitate loading. So successful was the transformation, it earned Austin Rover an award from the Design Council.

Two factors were seen to be key in the failure of the Montego to set the market alight – it never bettered its position as third in the marketplace behind the Sierra and Cavalier, and

Marketing-led 1.6L and Si attempted to rejuvenate Montego's image.

even then many of its sales were to fleets. Firstly, it had a dowdy image caused no doubt by styling that had been effectively set in the previous decade and second, the Austin brand was seen as undesirable when compared to Ford or Vauxhall. During 1987 the company set about trying to rectify both of these issues, starting in January with the launch of two new models – the Montego 1.6L and the Montego Si – with the same drive train as the MG. Each of these offered two-tone paintwork, maroon bumper inserts and maroon interior highlights in a bid to appeal to a younger section of the market. From the June 1987 facelift, the L would also be available in 2.0 form. A strong marketing campaign spearheaded by ex-Ford ad man Kevin Morley helped, with cars pirouetting through car parks courtesy of stunt driver Russ Swift.

The June facelift saw the first new changes implemented to the basic design. New deeper rubbing strips were fitted, while the dashboard switch layout was subtly modified. There was increased colour coding, and the 365mm metric wheels gave way to 14-inch imperial replacements. The Mayfair model gained the EFi engine from the Vanden Plas, while the L was now available with the 2.0 engine. Austin badges were missing from the boot lid but still present on the steering wheel and radiator grille, though these would be replaced by November with badges bearing the model name instead.

In this form, the Montego range would continue until its more comprehensive facelift of 1988, which we will cover in another chapter. This facelift was radically scaled back from the initial plan to revise the Montego with a new body aping the larger 800 model, codenamed 'AR9'. Only the grille would survive from AR9, and this would form a large part of the new model's appearance.

Above: The 1987 mid-term facelift brought deeper rubbing strips and additional colour coding.

Below: 1987 also saw imperial wheels replace the 365mm metric units.

AUSTIN ROVER

MONTEGO 1·6/2·0 HL ESTATE

Neg. No
-86-2064-86

4

SPORTING PRETENSIONS: MG

MG was a brand built upon the principles of badge engineering and sporting development of mainstream models – whatever the popularity of the MGB would have you think. And while plans for an MG Mini never came to fruition, it was inevitable that BL would seek to avoid the royalties associated with the Cooper name for the launch of its sporting Metro. The MG Metro proved a success, and it was felt within BL that the Maestro and Montego would benefit from similar treatment.

The Maestro was the first to get the MG treatment, with the MG Maestro 1600 available from launch. As the range-topping model, it received the optional digital dashboard as

MG Maestro 1600 was the first attempt at a performance model.

standard, with a red graphic pattern across the binnacle to indicate that this was a sporting model. The seats were trimmed in distinctive fabric, and red carpets and seat belts were fitted. Outside the car gained spoilers and 14-inch alloy wheels, while under the bonnet the 1.6-litre R-series was fitted with a pair of Weber 40DCNF carburettors on a unique inlet manifold. 0–60 could be achieved in 9.6 seconds, while the car would hit a maximum speed of 111 mph.

The second MG to be launched would follow in April 1984 when the Montego was launched; the MG Montego EFi would sit above the Vanden Plas in the range. Like the MG Maestro 1600, it would receive chin and tail spoilers, plus alloy wheels – this time, 365mm with TD rims – and an MG spec interior with red carpets and belts. Door handles, as with the Maestro, were black as opposed to the chrome of upmarket Austins, and the chrome window trims were omitted. Under the bonnet sat a fuel-injected version of the same O-series fitted in carburettor form to the standard models, while the gearbox employed unique close ratio gearing. This meant 115 bhp, 0–60 in 8.7 seconds and 115 mph. The MG Montego would be the only Montego model to be fitted with a digital dashboard, though this would be discontinued at the start of 1985. It is worth noting here that in 1988

Above: MG Montego EFi featured additional spoilers and standard alloy wheels.

Right: Later MG EFis gained imperial alloy wheels, shortly before wheel trims were standardised for the 2.0i.

Austin Rover produced a single MG Montego estate for evaluation, based on a Mayfair but trimmed inside and out to MG standards. It was never productionised for the UK, though some markets were offered an MG estate without fuel injection.

The introduction of the Montego meant that the new S-series engine was available for fitment to the Maestro range, and from July 1984 the MG Maestro 1600 was fitted with the new S-series engine. This would be short-lived, however, as October 1984 would bring a new development – the MG Maestro EFi. Easily distinguished from outside by its new grille with thicker bars and from behind the wheel by a new three-spoke steering wheel taken from the Montego, the MG Maestro EFi was as simple a concept as it sounded. The O-series from the MG Montego EFi was fitted under the Maestro's bonnet, offering greater power and torque than the 1.6 and 0–60 in 8.4 seconds. The digital dashboard would be retained into 1986, but would subsequently be replaced with the analogue unit fitted to later Montegos.

The next new model would be introduced for April 1985 as MG's fastest production model – the Montego Turbo. From outside this car could be distinguished from the humble EFi by its colour-coded door mirror cappings and door handles, larger boot spoiler and colour-coded front air dam in the manner of that fitted to the larger Rover Vitesse. Inside, the Turbo had unique seat trim. In this installation, the 2.0 O-series reverted to a carburettor, but was force-fed by a Garrett AiResearch T3 turbocharger offering up to 10 psi of boost. 150 bhp was the result, enough for 0–60 in 7.3 seconds and 126 mph.

The sole prototype MG Montego estate, pictured in 2004.

Above: For 1984 the Maestro gained the EFi engine too.

Below: MG Montego Turbo would be the fastest ever production MG at launch.

MG Maestro EFi looked good when compared to the Golf GTi and Escort XR3.

As part of a range rationalisation in June 1987 the specifications of the MG models changed. All lost their red seatbelts and red carpets, while both the Maestro and Montego EFi lost their alloy wheels in favour of wheel trims. 14-inch alloys of a new, concave disc design would be optional for both models. The Montego EFi gained the same air dam and boot spoiler as the turbo model. There was also a new name – the MG Maestro 2.0i and MG Montego 2.0i.

The following year both the Maestro and Montego would be realigned into the Rover range, and both models received a revamp as a result. The Maestro and Montego badges were gone, to be replaced by MG 2.0i branding. There would be new velour trim, and the rubbing strips and spoilers would be fully colour coded. Both cars would receive alloy

1987 saw alloy wheels relegated to the options list and a new name – MG 2.0i.

Right: The 1988 facelift brought new alloys and colour-coded trim.

Below: By now, Rover's marketing was up to scratch.

The Golf GTi will be along in a second.

MG Maestro, 0-60 in 8·4 secs.   Golf GTi, 0-60 in 9·6 secs.

wheels as standard once again – this time a 15-inch cross-spoke design, with a 5.5-inch profile for the Maestro and a slightly wider 6-inch profile for the Montego. The Montego Turbo would now look identical to the EFi save for badging.

The last new model was one that enthusiasts had been anticipating since 1985, and one that Austin Rover had toyed with as early as 1986. The MG Maestro Turbo of October 1988, however, would not be a mass production model, but a limited edition with just 504

Left: 1988 saw a facelift for the MG Montego too, with 2.0i receiving Turbo spoilers.

Below: An Exclusive Body Styling kit was a rarely seen option.

production examples and one motor show car produced according to official records. Just four colours would be available – British Racing Green, Flame Red, White Diamond and Black – and the spec would largely be as per the standard MG 2.0i. Where it would differ most visibly was the fitment of the Exclusive Body Styling kit developed for the Maestro by Tickford. This meant side skirts, chunky, angular bumpers incorporating front driving lamps, and an additional tailgate spoiler above the rear window. If the Montego Turbo had been considered quick, the Maestro was something new; 0–60 in 6.7 seconds and a top speed of 128 made it Austin Rover's fastest-accelerating car, even if not the outright fastest. It would be the most powerful Maestro or Montego produced.

All MG variants would be discontinued for 1991, as Rover launched the 220GTi and 420GSi derivatives of the new R8 range. These would use the new sixteen-valve M-series engine developed from the O-series, offering greater power and a more modern chassis than the existing MG models. Rover would also offer the 220 Turbo Coupe from 1992, and turbocharged 220 hatchbacks and 420 saloons from 1993.

Above: MG Maestro Turbo was fast – even by supercar standards.

Right: One of the more extreme-looking hot hatches, just 505 were built.

5

THE WARM VARIANTS: SI, GTI, ADVANTAGE

While the MG Maestro and Montego enjoyed the sporting halo within the model ranges, they were not the only models offered with a performance bent.

The Montego Si was the first performance model not to wear the MG badge, launched in January 1987. It bore the lower specification door cards of the base and L models, though with sports seats similar to those fitted to the MG. It used its own trim materials, and was essentially offered as a lower specification model with the fuel-injected engine and close-range gearbox of the MG. Launched early in 1987 exclusively with two-tone paintwork, the Si also had the same alloy wheels as the MG, but with unique Si centre caps. From June, like the MG, the alloys gave way to wheel trims, again the same style as the MG but with Si branding. Alloy wheels would be a cost option from launch; initially 365mm, but the same 14-inch units as became optional for the MG from June 1987. Priced to sit alongside the 2.0HL, the Si appealed to individuals and fleets for whom performance

Part of Rover's marketing push was to introduce new, appealing models such as the Si.

The Si was pitched as an instinctive choice.

mattered more than specification, and it is believed that it was developed in part to appeal to police forces. In production for just eighteen months, Sis were never common – it is believed that just one survives on the roads of Britain at the time of writing.

In June 1988 the Montego range was revamped with new specifications, and new trims. New to the range – but sitting at a similar price point to the outgoing Si – was a new Montego, the GTi. Like the Si, this car had a small chin spoiler inherited from the pre-facelift MG EFi and a boot spoiler, steel wheels and a relatively low level of trim, but the EFi engine and close ratio gearbox of the MG. Targeted at fleet buyers, the GTi was a more popular model than its predecessor in no small part owing to a longer production life. Cross-spoke alloys were optional, but once again two-tone paintwork was standard on saloon models. The GTi was also made available as an estate – the only UK market estate to be offered with the close ratio gearing, and the only UK market estate to be marketed as a performance model. The GTi was discontinued in 1992.

One special edition model was also perceived as a sports model, despite having the same mechanical package as the largest-engined L models of its era. The Advantage was inspired by the world of tennis, in the manner of the Wimbledon special edition Princesses of the 1970s. The Maestro Advantage of 1990 was based on the 1.6L, but offered only with three choices of colour – Black, British Racing Green and Cherry Red. All had colour-coded rubbing strips with white inserts, colour-coded MG specification spoilers front and rear,

Montego Si (left) offered MG pace at a lower price.

Above left: The model lasted just eighteen months in production.

Above right: Sports seats but with L trimmings.

After the 1988 facelift, the Si's place was taken by the GTi model.

THERE'S ANOTHER ADVANTAGE YOU CAN'T SEE.

At last you can afford to drive the car with the look you've always wanted.

Punch through the traffic in an MG styled Metro with alloy wheels and turbo spoilers. Surge down the motorways in a Maestro with alloys plus race-bred MG spoilers

and suspension. Or breeze along the autobahns in a Montego with turbo spoilers, alloy wheels and the ultimate luxury of power assisted steering.

Needless to say, the whole Advantage Series comes complete with the usual creature comforts including sunroof and superb digital

three-band stereo radio and cassette player.

Looks like a million dollars? Absolutely – but that's where the Advantage you can't see comes in. The price.

Incredibly, for such a hi-spec package, the Advantage Series' low-spec prices are just

£6,999* for the Metro, £8,770* for the Maestro and a mere £10,320* for the Montego.

METRO·MAESTRO·MONTEGO

Advantage

THE LOOK WITHOUT THE PRICE.

Advantage special edition offered sporting looks at a cut price.

and off-white MG alloy wheels. Inside, there was unique trim, and the models were identified by scripted Advantage badges. The Montego Advantage was created in a similar mould; based on the Montego 2.0L, it was fitted with MG spoilers, colour-coded rubbing strips with white inserts, off-white MG wheels and unique trim. The same three colours were available: Black, British Racing Green and Cherry Red. Advantage models are rare today, and collectible as a result. Their body kits lent them a sporting air, despite their mainstream mechanicals.

Maestro Advantage was based on the 1.6L.

Montego Advantage was based on the 2.0L. Both models gained spoilers and alloys.

6

THE LAP OF LUXURY: MAYFAIR AND VANDEN PLAS

Like MG, Vanden Plas had been a name revived for the Austin Metro. Unlike MG, however, the name wasn't to be revived as a brand, but as a trim level to rival Ford's highly regarded Ghia models. The Metro Vanden Plas had been aimed at former customers of the Allegro-based Vanden Plas 1500, though it was evident from the specification that they were very different cars.

The Maestro and Montego would be offered in Vanden Plas form too, following the pattern established by the Metro but on a larger scale. The Maestro Vanden Plas, introduced

Above left: Vanden Plas was the luxury range-topper.

Above right: Early Vanden Plas offered wood cappings, LCD dash, and plush Raschelle trim.

in 1983 with the rest of the range, followed that formula. Sitting above the HLS and only ever offered as a 1.6, it offered bright mirror cappings and grille, unique wheel trims, chrome door handles and unique interior trim. The Raschelle fabric was plush, and while the LCD dashboard and walnut door cappings may have felt slightly at odds with each other the overall package was plush enough for most tastes. As time passed, the LCD dash was dropped in favour of an analogue option and the Raschelle gave way to Box Velvet, as it would in every Vanden Plas from the Metro to the Rover SD1. Colour schemes would also change, but the biggest specification change was to be found for 1986. Alongside the new dashboard inherited from the larger Montego came leather trim, Box Velvet now listed as a no-cost option for those who preferred it. The following year two-tone paint would become an option, and the wheel trims would be replaced with items similar to those now fitted to the Metro and the Rover 200 in Vanden Plas form. It was in this final form that the Maestro Vanden Plas would end production in 1988.

By 1988 the Vanden Plas had evolved, with most sporting duotone paint.

Leather trim became standard fitment from 1986.

The year 1984 saw a Montego Vanden Plas join the range at launch, much as had happened for Maestro. In this instance, it again shared the largest non-sports engine, the 2.0 O-series with single carburettor. Like the Maestro, it came with bright mirror cappings and unique wheel trims, but unlike the Maestro the bonnet lip was adorned with chrome above the grille. It was trimmed with Raschelle and with walnut fillets to the doors, but the Montego's digital dashboard was reserved for MG models along. The Vanden Plas in production would always be fitted with an analogue dash. For 1985 Austin Rover sent the Vanden Plas upmarket, when it launched the Vanden Plas EFi. Following in the tyre marks of the SD1 Vanden Plas EFi, the Montego was produced by fitting the engine from the MG into a car with trimmings above the standard Vanden Plas.

It was long believed that the Vanden Plas EFi was developed after the launch of the initial range, but in recent years a prototype has come to light with an early Vanden Plas interior, an EFi engine and digital dashboard, and a VIN number indicating that it was built as a 1984 model Vanden Plas EFi. Given that this spec differs so clearly from the car as launched, it's likely that this was a prototype constructed prior to the marketing department's input. Factory cars didn't get the digital dashboard, but they were fitted with the same metric alloy wheels as the MG, leather seats, and electric rear windows in addition to the fronts. There would also be an estate variant, though this would never be trimmed in leather. The Vanden Plas and Vanden Plas EFi sat alongside each other until 1986, when the carburetted model was dropped. For 1987 the Vanden Plas would gain new imperial alloy wheels and two-tone paint.

AUSTIN ROVER **AUSTIN MONTEGO VANDEN PLAS** Neg. No. 321865

Not for publication until
00.01 hours, 25th April, 1984

Above: Montego Vanden Plas as launched.

Below: An EFi offered leather seats, MG-style alloys and fuel injection from 1985.

Right: Montego Vanden Plas EFi interior a sumptuous place to be.

Below: As this late estate shows, from 1987 the Vanden Plas 2.0i gained new 14-inch alloys.

AUSTIN ROVER AUSTIN MONTEGO VANDEN PLAS EFi AUTOMATIC GEARBOX

AUSTIN ROVER MONTEGO VANDEN PLAS ESTATE CAR 2.0i

The year 1986 saw the discontinuation of both HLS models and the Montego Vanden Plas. All three cars were replaced by new variants of the Maestro and Montego called the Mayfair.

Broadly, these cars kept the specification of the 1985 model year Vanden Plas cars. The Maestro Mayfair could be differentiated from the 1985 Vanden Plas only through badging

Left: Maestro Mayfair was a luxury model at a lower price than the VP.

Below: Late models subsumed HL but still offered a good specification.

and the new dashboard. The Montego Mayfair was more complex. Available in 1.6 and 2.0 forms, it kept the earlier Vanden Plas specification chrome fittings, wheel trims and interior trim, while the estate was trimmed as the Vanden Plas EFi but without the rear electric windows or the chromed roof rails.

For 1987 the Maestro Mayfair range would expand to replace the Maestro HL, losing its walnut door cappings and gaining a 1.3-litre option, along with Montego HL-style wheel trims. The Montego Mayfair range would contract, with both 1.6 and 2.0 models discontinued and replaced by a model using the same drive train as the Vanden Plas EFi. This Mayfair EFi would gain imperial wheels, and with them the wheel trims used on the mid-range HL model.

The Maestro Mayfair was replaced by the Maestro SL for 1988, while the Montego Mayfair would be replaced by the GSi model. The Maestro SL kept the Mayfair's Box Velvet trim, choice of 1.3- and 1.6-litre engines, but the optional electric windows became standard. The Montego GSi had new trim, albeit still velvet, with the full interior revision

Early Montego Mayfair was trimmed as the outgoing carburetted Vanden Plas.

AUSTIN ROVER AUSTIN MONTEGO MAYFAIR

New 14-inch wheel trims and the fuel injected engine were fitted from 1987.

of the facelift Montego. It also gained the rear electric windows which had previously been the preserve of the Vanden Plas, alongside the VP's alloy wheels. An optional Executive upgrade pack, which incorporated leather seats and an improved radio, would indirectly replace the Montego Vanden Plas.

The Maestro was the unusual model here – the Metro Mayfair had been replaced by a GS model, while the Montego SL sat below the GSi in the range. The lack of a Maestro GS can perhaps be attributed to the introduction of the Rover R8 200 range – anyone seeking an upmarket hatchback would avail themselves of this range instead.

The end of Maestro and Montego Vanden Plas production in 1988 – along with that of the Metro – would mark the end of the brand on the British market. The rights in America had been retained by Jaguar, where the Jaguar Vanden Plas was marketed in place of the Daimler available on the European market. Coleman Milne would also use the Vanden Plas name, briefly, to denote a mildly stretched variant of the Rover 800.

Mayfair and Vanden Plas Montegos were replaced by variations of the new GSi in 1988.

7

THE DEMISE OF AUSTIN AND THE 1988 FACELIFT

The Maestro and Montego ranges had proven themselves to be effective cars viewed in isolation, even if their reputation was perhaps not as strong as it might have been. Market research conducted by Austin Rover in the 1980s suggested that, in part, the Austin name was responsible. It was seen as weak in the image conscious fleet market and the company – buoyed by its effective work withdrawing brands over the past decades – felt that the Austin name may prove to be a name too many too.

The integration of the former Triumph line into Rover had brought the latter name into the mass market and buyers were keen to indulge in what seemed like premium motoring at a sensible price. Over time, the group intended that the cars formerly built by Austin would be seen in a similar light. But with money tight for their replacement and a light facelift the order of the day, management was reluctant to damage the Rover name on the British market by associating it with these former Austin products.

The solution was simple. Austin Rover would do to the Metro, Maestro and Montego exactly what it had done to the Maxi, Mini and Princess in the 1970s; sell them as cars built by the parent group without the brand visible on the cars. The Maestro and Montego would be built and marketed by Rover, but wouldn't be branded as Rovers for the British market. The process began shortly after the June 1987 facelift of the Maestro and Montego ranges, which introduced deeper rubbing strips and a revised dash layout. By September, both brands had lost the Austin badge from their boot lid, though the steering wheel and grille badges would still say Austin. The next step, from approximately November 1987, would be to replace these badges too. Steering wheels got the model name against a black background, while on the grille it sat across the middle of the Austin Rover emblem. Within a year, this badging would change again.

The 1988 Maestro and Montego models were presented as new models, though in both cases the work amounted to little more than a facelift. There was a new colour palette for both, as well as new model designations for the majority of models. Key to this was the dropping of Austin-specific models such as the HL, Mayfair and Vanden Plas. In their place, the newly branded Rover Group introduced titles that would fit with the forthcoming R8 200 series. HL became SL, a model available for the larger 800. Mayfair and Vanden Plas

Left: Maestro facelift primarily offered new colours and trim. Seen here is an entry level Special.

Below: Montego saloon would gain a new grille and rear lights.

MONTEGO

Sporting. Powerful. Highly appointed.
The Montego. Designed for the driver
who demands more.

were subsumed into the Montego GSi, which offered cloth trim and alloy wheels but far less chromework than its predecessors.

Cosmetically, there was little to separate the Maestro range from its predecessor, save for a new grille badge identical to that on the steering wheel, the new colours, and maroon rubbing strip inserts in place of chrome. The MG 2.0i continued as before, but its rubbing strips would be colour coded and it would be fitted with new 15-inch cross-spoke alloy wheels. The range now consisted of metal bumper Special, plastic bumper L and SL, and range-topping MG 2.0i.

Montego, on the other hand, was given a facelift – even if it wasn't as comprehensive as had been planned. There was a new grille, along with new flat-faced rear lamps for the saloon, new wheel trims, and new seats. The dashboard layout was further revised to differentiate it from the Maestro. Its range remained somewhat wider – the 1.3 was dropped, leaving the 1.6 as the only base model – and all 1.6 Montegos now used the gearbox of the 2.0 rather than the gearbox used in the Maestro. Moving up the range, L remained, Si became GTi, HL became SL, and Mayfair became GSi. An Executive pack would replace the Vanden Plas. MG models continued as before, with both 2.0i and Turbo gaining colour coding, the Turbo spec chin spoiler, and a wider variant of the Maestro's

AUSTIN ROVER

MONTEGO 2.0 DSL
DIRECT INJECTION TURBO DIESEL
Embargoed until 0001 hours Sunday 16th October 1988

Neg. No.
8/88/2120/A4

All 1988 Montegos looked like this, with a grille aping that of the larger 800.

A GTi estate was introduced, a development of the MG estate prototype we saw in chapter 4.

cross-spoke alloys. New to the range was a pair of diesels, the DL and DSL models, based on the specification of the petrol L and SL.

Specification changes for 1991 saw the L become the LX, and SL become SLX – fitted with extra toys to combat the similar moves taken by both Ford and Vauxhall for their fleet specials. The GSi was dropped in 1992 in preparation for the launch of the new Rover 600. The previously special edition Countryman estate joined the range as a plush variant, offering greater equipment levels than the SLX with optional alloy wheels and the chin spoiler from the MG Turbo.

The BMW takeover of 1994 would prove to be the death knell for both the Maestro and Montego families – to say nothing of the fact that EEC emissions rulings would see the diesels, the most popular models in a range with dwindling sales, ruled illegal by the following year. By this point the cars were virtually hand built on a makeshift production line in the Cowley Body Plant, the former South Works factory having been demolished the year before. The last Montego – a Clubman Diesel saloon, autographed by the workers and on display at the British Motor Museum – was produced in December 1994. In total, 605,411 Maestros and 571,460 Montegos were produced.

A new dash layout saw revised switch positions – Maestro would get this for 1992.

8

THE DIESEL MODELS

Arguably the most popular Maestro and Montego models on the second-hand market were the diesels – models that enjoyed popularity when new too. The MDi unit was Austin Rover's first in-house diesel engine, developed by Perkins in the wake of the failed V8 diesel 'Iceberg' project. The plan had been for the Iceberg engine to be fitted to the Range Rover, Rover SD1 and Jaguar XJ series, but after problems with cooling and the logistical issues caused by splitting BL into separate companies, it was abandoned. BL bought in the VM Motori 2.4-litre diesel engine for the Range Rover and SD1, as seen subsequently in the Jeep Cherokee. Meanwhile, the other project Perkins had been working on for BL continued apace.

The diesel engine was developed with the help of Perkins Engines.

This was a diesel engine for BL's smaller vehicles, based around the design of the O-series overhead cam petrol unit that would be fitted to the Montego. Developed under the codename of Ferret, the dieselised O-series would become one of the world's first direct injection diesel units, and would first be seen in naturally aspirated form under the bonnet of the 1986 model year Maestro van. In July 1986, Austin Rover and Perkins made a joint announcement: two versions of the engine were now on sale. The Prima 65 was a naturally aspirated variant developing 65 bhp, while the Prima 80 was turbocharged and offered 80 bhp. The units were only the third direct injection units on the market, behind those used by Ford and Iveco in the Transit and the Daily. However, these engines were too large for all but the biggest vans and cars, and the Prima met the needs of the car and car derived van market perfectly.

Development of the Prima had begun in 1982, and the total cost of the project had been £227 million. This included the cost of refitting Austin Rover's Longbridge plant to create major components. The injection pump was driven by the cam belt, using relatively standard injection equipment. The combustion chambers created their bowls in the pistons, and the shape of the inlet port also contributed to the efficiency of the design. Between these two design features Perkins had solved the issues of mixing air and fuel thoroughly in a direct application.

In a market that was becoming ever more attracted to diesel (from 1 in 50 car-derived vans in 1983 to 1 in 3 by 1985), Austin Rover was bullish about its new engine's market prospects, claiming an economy advantage over any comparable indirect injection engine of 15 per cent. The direct injection method meant there was less change of unburned fuel contaminating the oil, and thus the service intervals could be longer. It also claimed that the engine was more responsive owing to direct injection design.

Perkins' Engineering Director Tony Downes was equally confident, stating that 'payback mileage compared with petrol engines is cut in half. Where it will take at least 32,000km (20,000 miles) to recover the extra cost of an IDI engine, the Prima's payback mileage will be about 16,000km (10,000 miles)'.

The Maestro diesel van was launched with the Prima 65 engine in September 1986, an engine that would also see service in the Freight Rover 200 series, derived from the Sherpa, as a replacement for the B-series diesel already in use.

The first application of the turbocharged Prima 80 was in 1988, when Rover fitted the engine to the Montego in time for the facelift. Diesel Montegos were made available in L spec and SL spec from launch, while upmarket models such as the GTi and GSi remained petrol-only. This would be the second diesel model available in the Rover Group range – in the same year Rover introduced the 825D as a belated replacement for the VM-engined SD1. Once again, the 800 used the VM engine, but came only in base spec and with the fastback body style. Montego meant a wider range of specifications and body styles, offering a saloon and estate to boot.

The Montego was the easier car to live with too. It may have been noisier than the 825D, but it offered vastly improved fuel economy and servicing intervals, making it an ideal car to target at the fleet market. The 12,000-mile service intervals and 70,000-mile cambelt interval were almost unheard of, and this longevity between maintenance meant that the Maestro and Montego diesel would remain desirable long after production finally ended in 1995.

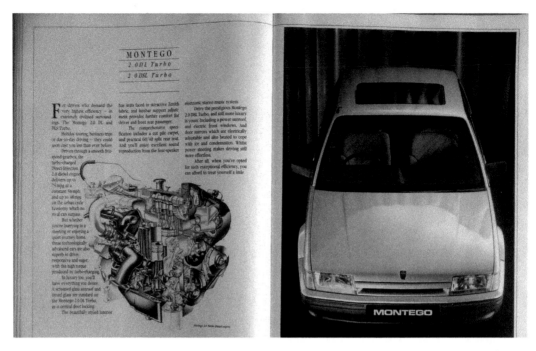

Montego was the first car to get the MDi engine, though it had been available in the van two years earlier.

The diesel Montego was only officially available with manual transmission; unlike today, the diesel automatic wasn't a popular option on the new car market and Rover didn't see fit to offer it as a production model. However, Perkins did experiment with the concept in prototype form. It is believed that six cars were built in total with diesel engines and automatic gearboxes, one of which survives. Such a model may have proved popular among taxi drivers; however, its place as a footnote in the Montego's history is that of an intriguing 'might-have-been'.

The Maestro would also be made available in diesel form – this time, with the Prima 65 that was already in service in the van. This would be replaced in 1992 with the Prima 80, as part of a careful rationalisation of the Maestro and Montego range once the Rover R8 had become established in the marketplace and ahead of the launch of the 600. The latter car would use a new diesel engine: the L-series – derived from the Prima, but designed and produced in house by Rover. Meanwhile, the R8 ranges abandoned the Prima engine line completely. Rover felt that the refinement of indirect injection would better suit what was to be pitched as a premium purchase, and bought XUD engines from Peugeot in France. These would also be used in the Sherpa van after EEC regulations rendered the Prima unviable for 1995.

The Montego diesel estate and the Maestro diesel became especially desirable second-hand buys. The two ranges were not best known for holding value, but the Maestro Clubman TD and the Montego Countryman TD in particular held their values better than any other Maestro or Montego model had managed. Even today they're desired by people as economic modern classics up to the rigours of daily use. While there is still a healthy conversion market for these engines to be fitted into Land Rover products, the scarcity of these models today means that the majority are now sold to enthusiasts rather than to breakers. A number of Maestros and Montegos have been fitted with the later L-series diesel, offering even greater performance and economy at the expense of originality.

Late Countryman diesel estates (left) are still desirable transport today.

9

REPLACING THE MAESTRO AND MONTEGO

The replacement of the Maestro and Montego ranges was by no means as clear cut as it ought to have been. In fact, it was almost as convoluted as the range that preceded them. Part of the cause for this can be laid at the door of Rover's burgeoning relationship with Honda, but arguably a greater part can be attributed to the increasing aspirations of the Rover brand and the higher prices the company sought to achieve as a result.

The biggest problem in determining the true line of succession was the existence of the first Rover 200 'SD3' – the replacement for the Triumph Acclaim. This series was an initial means of testing the waters prior to the true joint design venture, which would begin with the Rover 800 and Honda Legend. It meant that by offering a more compact yet upmarket

The Rover 200 (SD3) led to mid-market confusion in the 1980s.

alternative to the Maestro and Montego in its middle market, Austin-Rover had been able to appeal to a wider range of customers. The Acclaim had been a crucial model in the pre-Maestro era, when BL's middle range had been perceived as outdated the Acclaim provided not only an effective trial run for the future joint venture, but lent support to the existing range. The subsequent Rover 200 would continue this, with more of an emphasis upon its premium market position.

The problem with this is that when the successors to the Maestro, Montego and 200 were introduced at a similar time, there was little clarity as to precisely which of the newer cars was replacing which of the older designs.

The Rover R8 range makes a sensible place to begin in our assessment of Rover's attempts to succeed the Maestro and Montego, largely because in the eyes of the world this

Its replacement, the R8, seemed more suited to replacement of the Maestro...

...while the 400 saloon seemed a better replacement for the SD3.

was indeed the successor. Jointly developed between Rover and Honda, the project also begat the Concerto, and in Rover form utilised the then new K-series, the Honda D-series, and subsequently the M-series in 2.0 form. In 200 hatchback form it was launched in 1989, alongside the existing 200 saloon, which was then discontinued when the R8 400 saloon was launched the following year. It's possible, therefore, to draw the link between the R8 series and the SD3 – the Rover 200 saloon was supplemented by the 200 hatchback and supplanted by the 400 saloon.

Where things become more blurred, however, is that the Maestro range – while pared down slightly – was not discontinued until the R8 itself was nearing replacement in 1995. The Montego, likewise, survived until the mid 1990s – not only beyond the launch of the 400, but beyond the launch of the larger 600 too. While the 200 hatch might have been pitched as a Maestro replacement its upmarket pricing meant the continuation of the older model so as not to lose ground to the competition. This left the buying public confused, and with four cars on the market instead of three, it looked like Rover Group was returning to the range confusion of the late 1970s. The replacement of the Montego would cause similar issues.

The 600, codenamed 'SK1', was launched in 1993 and coincided with a slimming-down of the more upmarket portion of the Montego saloon range. Based on Honda's Accord, there was no direct successor to the Montego estate, but the 600 saloon competed in the same fleet car market that the Montego had enjoyed during the 1980s. Meanwhile, the Montego estate range was broadened. Montego saloon became a special order model from 1994, but the estate continued to 1995. By then Rover had introduced the 400 Tourer – a smaller

A late R8 – by this stage, Maestro was still available new from the same showrooms.

estate car targeted at the lifestyle market and without the seven-seat option that had made the Montego so popular among larger families. It would be as close to a Montego estate successor as Rover Group achieved until the new millennium.

By 1994, the mid-market range that had successfully shrunk to three a decade earlier was now back up to five separate model ranges across three families: Maestro, Montego, 200, 400 and 600. Only when the 200 and 400 were replaced by the new 400 hatch and saloon

Right: The 600 was a fine Montego replacement, but offered no estate.

Below: A little clarity was restored in 1995 – Maestro, Montego and R8 all replaced by HH-R 400.

ROVER GROUP   THE NEW ROVER 400 SERIES SALOON AND 5DR   RGS/0296/715

A Rover Group Product Communications (0121 782 8000) photograph. Copyright free for editorial purposes only. For any other use, prior written permission is required.

series for 1995 – and the Maestro and Montego finally discontinued – did the confusion become clearer, with a return to a three-model line-up in the middle range. This would comprise two families: 400 hatch, 400 saloon and 600 saloon. These models would further be rationalised into the Rover 45 and 75 ranges.

Because of the premium positioning of the Rover brand, the Maestro and Montego were forced to continue beyond the introduction of their effective successors. It was as if once the Austin brand was withdrawn Rover wasn't sure how to reconcile the needs of the Maestro customer with the company's more prestigious image and, in the absence of a definite plan, chose to continue production for as long as it felt practical.

The Rover 75 would replace the 600 in due course. An estate would be offered once more.

10

VAN ORDINAIRE, THE COMMERCIAL MAESTROS

The car-derived van sector was a big part of the plan for the Maestro. During the 1970s, the Morris Marina-based vans were popular alternatives to the Ford Escort van and various offering from Vauxhall sister brand Bedford, and though the Ital-based 575 series had lasted well it was clear that there would need to be a new van based upon the Maestro. Ford's Mk3 Escort van of 1981 changed the game for light vans; it was front-wheel drive with a correspondingly lower-load floor and also integrated a raised roof. The Bedford Astravan offered the former, but not the latter – that would be the preserve of the Astramax of 1986.

Maestro van was basic but commodious.

While the discontinuation of the older, cheaper Bedford HA meant that there were fleet orders from the Post Office and the AA for the Morris 575, it was clear that a new van would be needed. By April 1984 Austin Rover was running down its stock of Ital vans, and just six months later the Maestro van was unveiled at the 1984 Birmingham Motor Show. There would be two models and two different engines. The Maestro 500 van could carry 500 kg, while the stronger Maestro 700 could carry 700 kg. All vans were powered by A-series engines, though unlike the outgoing model the smallest size was the 1,275cc unit used in the car. This was in fact the standard engine in car-derived 69 bhp specification, though a lower-compression unit developing 62 bhp was available for companies who preferred to use cheaper two-star petrol in their fleets. Everything behind the A posts was new, with the exception of the doors. There were new side pressings, a higher roof, twin rear doors and a unique corrugated floor for strength, giving an overall load are of almost 86 cubic feet – 6 more than the Escort. There was a dead axle at the back, unique to the vans, with single leaf springs. The hubs were sturdier and utilised the larger 4×4.5-inch stud spacing of the Ambassador range. The braking system included a limiting valve to prevent rear wheel lock on unladen examples.

Cosmetically, the vans differed from the cars in detail. They used the same metal bumpers as the base, but with a black radiator grille and black surrounds hiding generic

AUSTIN ROVER

MAESTRO 500 L 2.0 DIESEL VAN
Embargoed until 0001 hours Sunday 16th October 1988

Neg. No.
9.88/2127/F3

Press images focused on its business potential.

Lucas headlamps of the type used on the Allegro. These were seen as a cheaper solution than the shaped lamps of the Maestro hatch, and easier to replace should they be damaged. A manual choke was fitted for simplicity, and lower final drive ratios were used for improved acceleration when laden. The 500 van used 13-inch wheels similar to those used on the Maestro car, while 700 vans used a larger 14-inch wheel with reinforced tyres.

Continuing the theme of twos, there would be two trim specifications and two trim colours. The base City had vinyl seats, while the L offered cloth seats, a radio, a cigar lighter and intermittent wash wipe. In both instances, trim was available in Bitter Chocolate or Flint Grey. Production would begin in January 1985, and within just three months Austin Rover had 25 per cent of the car-derived van market – sitting just behind Ford at 32 per cent. For 1986 Austin Rover facelifted the van with the new dashboard from the Montego saloon, taking the same opportunity to introduce side repeaters and to change the grille finish from black to silver. At the same time it expanded the range with the fitment of the 1.6-litre S-series to the 700 City van as an option – again, in high- and low-compression

Advertisements targeted the self-employed professional.

Austin Rover's car-derived vans competed with Ford and Bedford.

variations. Never popular, the 1.6-litre van would be discontinued just three years later. Meanwhile, in October of the same year Austin Rover launched the Maestro 500 City and 700 City in diesel form, using the naturally aspirated Prima 65 variant of its MDi engine. The first fleet order was for 100, from the Post Office, in November 1986 – in the same period almost 800 Escort vans had been ordered by the same customer. During flagging sales Austin Rover would introduce L variants of the diesel vans in February 1987. That same year the van became available for the first time in left-hand drive in France, Belgium, Spain, Portugal and the Netherlands – all markets where diesel offered a distinct advantage.

But from here, the newly named Rover Group had little time for the Maestro van, which had been kept in production while it generated a profit – a replacement wasn't considered as it was felt that commercial vehicles sat uncomfortably within what was becoming a premium brand's range. By 1992 Rover ceased production of the Metro van, leaving the Maestro as its sole car derived commercial model. For this model year, the 1.3 was fitted with a catalytic converter, but would be discontinued entirely in 1993. That left just the diesel models – in 500 and 700 form – and by now using the dashboard of the facelifted Montego, which had filtered down into the Maestro range. In June 1994, Rover announced that production would cease in the following month after ten years of manufacture. Not only was the van a poor fit with the new range, but EEC emissions legislation would render the Prima non-compliant by the start of 1995. There would be no further car-derived vans from the company until the launch of the Rover 25-based Commerce in 2003.

THE MAESTRO VAN RANGE

	1.3LC	1.3HC	1.6LC	1.6HC	2.0D
500 CITY	●	●			●
500 L	●	●			●
700 CITY		●	●	●	●
700 L		●			●

Twelve models were available by 1987.

11

THE CONVERTERS: MAESTRO AND MONTEGO SPECIALS

Banham 200

Paul Banham is a name that is well known in the kit car world. He created a XJS facelift, which gave the car an E-type appearance, produced Metro-based previews of the Audi TT, and chopped the roofs from Series XJs and XJCs. It should come as no surprise that when he was invited to purchase the original tooling for the Ford RS200, he jumped at the idea of producing a rally replica that could be sold in kit form.

The Banham 200 was a Maestro under the skin.

What wouldn't be on offer though, would be the chassis or engine – so there would be no all-wheel drive Cosworth power for his new RS200 replicas. Banham considered the popular cars available for little money second hand and hit upon the Austin Maestro as a worthwhile donor, which offered a similar road footprint to the RS200. It should be relatively easy, he reasoned, to sit the shell from the RS200 atop a Maestro. And with plenty of MG EFis about, the result shouldn't exactly hang about.

Not that there's anything to stop people producing RS200s based around the mechanicals of the MG Maestro 1600, or even a 1.3HLE. But the performance appeal of the car meant that Banham envisaged the majority of donor cars being MG Maestro EFis, or even Montego Turbos. The basic Maestro structure is retained under the RS200 shell – the Maestro being stripped of any outer panels and any aspects of the shell that would impede the fitment of the RS200 body. This means that where the RS200 would have kept its engine, there's space for the original Maestro's rear seat or a considerable amount of luggage, making this a Group B replica the whole family can enjoy.

It's possible to retain the Maestro dash, though most of Banham's clientele opted for one more in keeping with the original RS200 unit. Banham produced the RS200 replicas between 2000 and 2004, and it's believed that just a handful of cars were built.

Coleman Milne Warwick and Hebden

Traditionally, funeral cars in Britain in the 1980s would be large Vauxhalls or large Fords. But there was a market for something smaller at the budget end of the market – a funeral car that could achieve a price tag, when built, of under £20,000. Conversion would eat a huge chunk of that, necessitating an inexpensive base car. Coleman Milne's budget-conscious subsidiary Woodall Nicholson had previously converted Princesses into funeral limousines and hearses, the Kirklees and the Hebden. It felt that a similar project based around the new Montego would be a viable option as an entry-level model. The Warwick and the new Hebden were the result. Stretched by 30 inches, the 17-foot 2-inch frame on each of them would dwarf a Jaguar XJ. And while the Hebden's styling was typical of the hearse market, the Warwick showed that if anything the Montego's awkward styling suited the limousine length better than it did the standard saloon. The Hebden was 9 inches taller than a standard Montego; the Warwick's height was unchanged from the donor.

The Warwick had a double market, of course. Away from the carriage trade it was targeted at those who required dignified and extended chauffeur transport on a budget – company chairmen, for instance, or local authorities as mayoral transport. A standard Montego 2.0 would be supplied to Woodall Nicholson, minus certain items of interior trim. The car would be sawn in half and mounted on a jig, which would be used to bolster the portions until a new centre section could be welded in. This would incorporate reinforcements designed to hold the shell stiff at its new length. The conversion could take up to three months, and as it had gained Type Approval it wouldn't affect the car's standard factory warranty.

Woodall Nicholson's brochures were not fulsome in their promotion of the car. Sharing page space with sister company Coleman Milne, its Granada conversions occupied four

Left: Montegos made excellent funeral cars.

Below: Woodall Nicholson marketed the Warwick and Hebden.

Specifications

	Dimensions Overall			GVW kg	Engine Size	Gearbox	Steering	Brakes	Wheels	Tyres
	Length	Width	Height							
Dorchester	18' 0½"	6' 5½"	5' 2"	2.06 tons	2.8 EFI	4 speed AUTO	PAS	ABS	Alloy 15 x 6J	195 x 65 VR
	5.500 m	1.969 m	1.575 m	2100 kg						
Cardinal	18' 0½"	6' 5½"	5' 10"	2.06 tons	2.8 EFI	4 speed AUTO	PAS	ABS	Alloy 15 x 6J	195 x 65 VR
	5.500 m	1.969 m	1.778 m	2100 kg						
Rosedale	18' 0½"	6' 5½"	5' 2"	2.06 tons	2.8 EFI	4 speed AUTO	PAS	ABS	Alloy 15 x 6J	195 x 65 VR
	5.500 m	1.969 m	1.575 m	2100 kg						
Norwood	18' 0½"	6' 5½"	5' 8½"	2.06 tons	2.8 EFI	4 speed AUTO	PAS	ABS	Alloy 15 x 6J	195 x 65 VR
	5.500 m	1.969 m	1.740 m	2100 kg						
Warwick	17' 2"	6' 5½"	4' 9"	1.77 tons	2.0	3 speed MAN	PAS	SERVO	Alloy 14 x 5½J	180 x 65 TD
	5.232 m	1.969 m	1.448 m	1800 kg						
Hebden	17' 2"	6' 5½"	5' 5"	1.77 tons	2.0	3 speed MAN	PAS	SERVO	Alloy 14 x 5½J	180 x 65 TD
	5.232 m	1.969 m	1.646 m	1800 kg						
Daimler DS420	18' 10"	6' 6"	6' 2"	2.24 tons	4.2	3 speed AUTO	PAS	SERVO	Steel 15 x 6J	235 x 70 HR
	5.740 m	1.980 m	1.880 m	2286 kg						

Warwick and Hebden were pitched as entry level models.

times the brochure space of the Montegos, which felt tacked in as a last-minute addendum. But as a budget alternative it did remain available beyond the Montego facelift of 1989. Barely a handful of Montegos were converted, including, it's believed, three MGs. No Warwicks are known to survive, and only a couple of Hebdens are still known at the time of writing.

12

POST-PRODUCTION MAESTROS: RODACAR

Rover Group had traditionally been good at farming out its unwanted cast-offs come the end of production. The Hindustan Ambassador was after all a Morris Oxford, rebadged and re-engineered (and reintroduced to Britain as the Fullbore in the 1990s). The Standard Gazel had been a Triumph Herald modified with four doors and a new tail for the Indian market. The executive Standard 2000 in India was a Rover SD1 with a Standard Vanguard engine, and the Chinese had been sold the rights to the Morris Ital. It was no surprise that Rover wanted to sell off the rights to the Maestro, inviting offers from a number of interested parties.

One of the cars assembled at Parkway Services, Ledbury.

These cars were broadly to Clubman specification.

The successful bid was from a group led by the Bulgarian government to set up a knock-down assembly plant on the Black Sea coast at Varna. Known in the UK as Project Enterprise, the commissioning of the factory was also to be led by Rover's people. Eight Cowley employees and two from British Aerospace were sent to the proposed Varna site with the aim of establishing a factory. Investment estimates of $20 million meant that this would be the biggest foreign investment in Bulgaria since the end of the Cold War.

Building the factory would begin in late 1994, and by June 1995 the first cars were being built by the new Rodacar enterprise. Rodacar stood for Rover/Daru – the companies that owned Rodacar with 51 per cent Rover holding and the rest by Daru. Daru was the main agent for BMW in Bulgaria, meaning it could offer local sales expertise and outlets for Rover's product. The specification of the Rodacar Maestro was simple and akin to the entry-level Clubman with metal bumpers, no sunroof, but fitted with the lower-ratio van gearbox and the 14-inch wheels from the Clubman diesel to raise the ground clearance and offer swifter acceleration. The factory was officially opened by Bulgarian President Zhelyu Zhelev on 8 September 1995.

Despite the project meeting budget, cost and volume targets, it ultimately proved to be unsuccessful. The cars met the same quality standard as British Maestros as a minimum,

All were 1.3, albeit with diesel-spec 14-inch wheels for added ground clearance.

but a weak sales and marketing strategy meant that the market simply wasn't aware of the car's virtues. Tragedy had struck the Varna project in 1995 when one of Rodacar's key people was killed in a road accident. He had been the only link between the project and the Bulgarian government, and without his input many of the concessions that had been agreed evaporated. The Bulgarians had agreed to reduce import duty on the parts imported from Britain until local manufacture would be viable, and without this the Maestro would simply prove too expensive to build. This would also result in the abandonment of plans to produce a diesel variant of the Rodacar Maestro – the levies on imported engines would prove insurmountable.

When Volkswagen was able to import the Skoda Felicia from Czechoslovakia at just half the import duty levied on the knock-down Maestro parts from Britain, the Rodacar project would prove to be dead in the water. The Skoda was more modern, cheaper, and had better support in mainland Europe than the cast-off 1980s relic Rover was peddling. The Bulgarian government had also placed orders for thousands of Maestros as official cars – orders it would subsequently refuse to confirm.

Parkway Services assembled vans too. (Image courtesy kitmasterbloke, CC BY 2.0)

Just 2,200 cars would be built before the factory doors closed on 4 April 1996, with 250 jobs lost. Of the 2,200 cars, barely 200 had been sold in Bulgaria.

However, this would not prove to be the end of the Rodacar story, because two different companies would purchase the remnants and reimport the Maestro to Britain to be sold on. Best known of these is Parkway Services, a garage in Ledbury that procured 621 knock-down Maestro kits and assembled them using right-hand drive conversion kits sourced initially from Rover and subsequently from scrapyards when the supply of brand new parts dried up.

All cars were produced to a single specification and in a choice of four colours – black, white, red or blue. The conversion would use a right-hand drive steering rack, column, dashboard and wipers, and cars would be fitted with speedometers registering in miles per hour. Registered as kit cars when new, they could be had on the latest registration – we know of the production of at least two Ledbury-built Maestros that ended up registered on 2001 51 plates. At £4,995, between 1998 and 2001 the Maestro would enjoy the honour of being Britain's cheapest new car – and, so far as we can find, the only new car still to be sold with a carburettor. The final cars, sold with left-hand drive, are registered in the G***LWP series.

Apple 2000 Limited of Bury St Edmonds was the other company to import former Rodacar Maestros. It, however, imported cars that had been completed by Rodacar. These cars are typically given age-related registrations, and unlike the Parkway cars retain Rover Group VIN numbers as they were completed by Rover at the Rodacar facility. These cars can be identified by left-hand drive specification wipers and mirrors.

Apple 2000 offered cars that had already been built and reimported.

13

POST-PRODUCTION MAESTROS: CHINESE PRODUCTION

The failure of the Bulgarian project was not the end of the road for the Maestro project. While Rodacar may have failed, Rover Group was not new to recycling its products for developing markets. Attempts to market the Montego in India would also fail, leaving the pair open for further deals should they be desired elsewhere. Seeing an opportunity, it turned to a nation that was already enjoying the former fruits of Leyland labours.

Chengdu Auto Works, a subsidiary of First Auto Works (remember this name, it'll come in later), was already building the Huandu CAC6430, and had been since 1998. The Huandu was effectively a re-engineered version of the Morris Ital, available in estate, van and pickup variations, plus a five-seat van. The Ital-based Huandu range sat on slightly higher suspension in acknowledgement of rural China's poor roads, had a new front bumper, and used locally produced engines in place of the A-series and O-series of the British original. Earlier in the decade, Rover had worked directly with Chengdu to produce a trio of prototype cars with the Sherpa's O-series engine and five-speed gearbox in a bid to develop the Ital for its new market. The Huandu might not have been an especially strong seller, but it paved the way for some more interesting deals.

Tobacco company Etsong spent 1998 building a factory for its own attempt at car and van production: the Lubao. After the failed ventures in Bulgaria and India, Rover had sold the tooling for both the Maestro and Montego to RDS International, which sold it in turn in 1997 to the Etsong Tobacco Company for £11 million. The following year Etsong bought the intellectual property necessary to build the cars – a vital element missing from the earlier tooling deal. Etsong, it is believed, bought the original tooling for all Maestro and Montego models, though the Montego saloon and estate were not mass produced in China. Reports online suggest that one saloon and one estate were constructed for assessment purposes, though it remains unclear whether these were cars built locally or imported as examples of the finished product.

The first Lubaos were built in May 1999 – a pair of vans with Toyota engines to use as development prototypes ahead of the range's 2000 launch. A year after the Lubao QE6440's launch, Etsong offered a car variant – the QE6400, which used the shell of the five-door Maestro. Etsong didn't have the necessary licence to build cars in China – a matter neatly circumvented by registering the Lubao as a five-seat bus to be produced for

Etsong initially produced the Maestro Van as the Lubao CA6440.

local consumption, but one which prevented its sale across China as a whole until it could be rectified. Etsong did not enjoy popularity as a result – few Lubaos were sold, and the company was eventually taken over by First Auto Works – whose subsidiary had produced the Huandu-branded Ital. This opened up the possibility of sales of the newly named CA6410UA hatchback all over China as a car – FAW had a licence to produce and sell cars, so Etsong capitalised on this newfound legal ability to market them. The van would be renamed the FAW Jiefang CA1020, while a five-seat van was offered as the FAW Jiefang CA6440UA. The car would continue as the FAW Jiefang CA6400UA.

On 11 May 2003, some twenty years after the Maestro had been launched, it finally received a meaningful facelift. FAW fitted the Montego front end to the Jiefang range, reinstating the Lubao name for the car variant – now called the CA6410UA in acknowledgement of the extra length of the Montego nose. Both saloon and van variants looked awkward in side profile, owing to the differing wheel arch depths of the Maestro and Montego wings, but as a simple and effective facelift it is undeniable that it succeeded in making the car look appreciably different.

These cars still appear to have been produced by Etsong, under the guidance of parent company FAW and bearing FAW branding. But from December 2003, a joint venture was formed – the FAW Etsong Qingdao Automobile Co. Ltd – with 60 per cent owned by FAW and 40 per cent by Etsong. Just 3,000 Maestros were made by Etsong and FAW before the tooling and rights were sold once again in 2008, to Sichuan Yema Automobile Co.

Above: Later models gained Montego-style noses.

Below: Production of these hybrids began in 2003.

Further facelifts, but Maestro origin still clear.

The final development was this six-door, high-roofed van.

Yema did not produce the CA6410UA or any other Maestro- or Montego-based cars, but maintained production of the van as the Yema SQJ6450. The passenger variant of the van was produced as the SQJ6450N. Yema would also develop a seven-seat van with a higher roof, unusual in that it also incorporated side doors to the rear. This Maestro mini MPV was the last car to use a full Maestro-based shell, but Yema would continue to use the Maestro and Montego underpinnings and sections of their design for years to come as part of more modern models.

Above: Yema F99 was a Maestro under the skin.

Below: F99 bore a strong resemblance to the Subaru Forester SUV.

Maestro window frame shape is clearly visible from this angle.

Resembling a shortened Subaru Forester, the Yema F99 of 2009 was heavily based on the underpinnings of the Maestro-based SQJ6450 range. It used the Maestro floor pan, albeit with more modern engines, and while information on the subject is understandably lacking, it certainly appears that the F-series uses the same door glass and possibly even door shells as the Austin Maestro. The F99 would be supplemented by the F10 in 2011 – a similar concept with an Audi-aping radiator grille. The same year would also see the F12 launched, which was based upon the F10 but with marginally different exterior treatment. These cars would be produced to 2014. The Yema F16, launched at that year's Chengdu Auto Show, would be a further facelift of the original Maestro-based design. Production appears to have ceased for good in 2017.

Above: The F99 would be facelifted into the F12.

Below: F16 offered a more modern slant on the same design.

14

POST-PRODUCTION MONTEGOS: SIPANI

The Maestro wasn't the only model to be sent overseas – the Montego would be offered the chance to live on on the other side of the world too. But owing to the terms of the deal brokered, the plan ultimately faltered, with just a couple of hundred examples sold.

Sipani had its roots in Sunrise Automotive Industries. This company, founded in 1974, had spent its early years producing three-wheeled rickshaws before agreeing to licence build the Reliant Kitten as the Sipani Dolphin in 1982. Light and powerful by Indian standards, it earned a reputation as an unlikely performance car. Only 1,976 Dolphins were built over a five-year period – a far cry from the 6,000 per year projected. In part, this was because the Indian government had imposed restrictions on Sipani, forcing it to sell the Dolphin solely in southern India. The Suzuki-based Maruti 800 prompted a revised Dolphin – the Sipani Montana, with five-door bodywork as an option and a larger body. That in turn began the Sipani D-1, which with its Mahindra- and Autoland-sourced parts could claim to be a 100 per cent locally sourced and built vehicle.

Sipani had struck a deal with Rover to assemble the Montego in a bid to move upmarket into a potentially more profitable market sector. The idea was that saloons and estates would be exported in a semi-knocked-down state, to be finished and sold by Sipani and

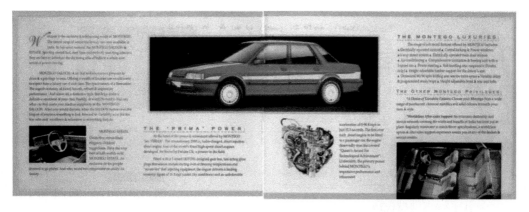

Indian Montego had its own brochure.

Above: Sipani Motors had been better known for the Reliant-based Dolphin.

Below: The Hindustan Ambassador was old tech, but proven and cheap.

its subsidiary Dolphin Motors Ltd. These cars had been built in 1994, and only really required the installation of air conditioning and minor components to be complete cars. But customs clearance wasn't forthcoming, despite Sipani having negotiated a deal with the government that clearance would be available for these early cars, and later models would gradually assume a greater quantity of local content. The long-term aim was to build the cars completely in India.

These difficulties meant that the car was no longer economically viable, but Sipani persisted, launching the car under the Rover Montego name to distance it in the minds of buyers from the previous Reliant-based city cars for which Sipani had become known. Higher duties meant that there was no alternative but to sell the car for as much as Rs678,000 – in a market where the Maruti 800 could be had for barely a tenth of the money and even a Hindustan Ambassador would have cost under Rs100,000. Granted, there was no Hindustan estate, but you needed Rs725,000 if the Montego estate proved tempting...

When tested by *Auto India* in 1994, the Montego earned praise, though writers were dubious about the Sipani brand.

We expect to receive a great deal of flak from doubters of the Montego's arrival on Indian roads. Sipani is a bad word for many of our readers. But although there's no doubt that Sipani's credibility as a car manufacturer remains suspect, the Montego project is Sipani's one chance to come and clean and we feel he should be able to pull it off.

Its dynamic qualities were found to be pleasing.

In terms of road manners, the Montego, again, is on a different plane, striking a find balance between handling and ride for this class of car. Though it does not have the agility or quick reflexes to dart into corners on twisty roads like a smaller, lighter car, it tackled bends with remarkable fluency... If performance were to be the Montego's main story then its fuel efficiency makes the headlines. The Montego's fuel economy sets new standards of stinginess, and when you consider that this is done with a 2-litre turbo engine, the achievement is almost ludicrous. In practical terms, the Montego is possibly the most economical car to run.

The cars were to what amounted to Clubman TD specification, and both saloons and estates were available. Compared with cars like the Hindustan Ambassador and even the upmarket Hindustan Contessa, the Montego would have seemed up to date, but market forces conspired against it. First of these was General Motors, which established a factory in India to build Daewoo Nexia/Cielo models locally. Even at a third of the price of the Montego the Daewoo couldn't outsell the Ambassador, but highlighted the Montego as effectively overpriced. But key to the model's failure was the price forced upon it by the refusal to relax the import duty until local production could be assumed. Sipani needed the revenue from sales to invest in production, and without that money it was unable to produce enough locally to reduce the prices to a more affordable level. This Catch-22 situation would ultimately sabotage the Montego in India from the very first example to the very last. In its first full year, Sipani sold fewer than 250 Montegos in India, and this was the model's best

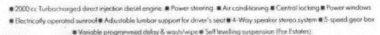
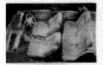

The Montego may have offered 'pure luxury', but it came at a hefty price.

year in terms of sales. Just 500 semi-knocked-down Montegos were exported – half of which were estates – and it took until 1998 for dealers to sell the last of them.

Part of the problem was that Sipani's dealer network was small and unsophisticated, and customers with the sort of money that would be necessary to buy a Montego didn't want to deal with back street workshops when they could enjoy a slicker dealership experience elsewhere. The Indian customer was also growing more sophisticated, and while the Ambassador was still at the forefront of the market it was clear that the Montego was a European cast off, and while it wasn't out of date when compared with the Premier Padmini there were still more modern alternatives available for a smaller outlay.

Dolphin Motors was rebranded as Dars Automobiles in 2000, and now specialises in LPG conversion rather than automotive manufacture.

Just 250 saloons and 250 estates were sold.

15

BUYING A MAESTRO OR MONTEGO TODAY

Buying a Maestro or Montego today is more difficult than ever, primarily because the number of available cars has dwindled since production ceased and partly because incentive schemes such as the 2008 Scrappage Scheme in Britain saw many cars of the 1980s and 1990s forcibly retired from the road. In addition, because of their rarity there are no dedicated model specialists, and neither panels nor trim are being remanufactured to enable restoration. This, however, shouldn't be enough to dissuade the ardent from purchase.

Rust will be the biggest killer of any Maestro or Montego you might wish to buy. Particular areas of concern are the wheel arches and sills, which can trap water. Major corrosion here will be difficult to fix properly, though on the front wheel arches at least there if the benefit of bolt-on wings for rapid replacement. A-pillars rust where they meet the roof panel, and you can expect corrosion across the top of the front screen on all cars,

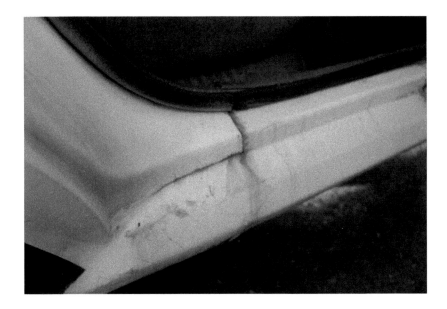

Rot in the sill to rear arch seams can get expensive.

Left: The front wing joint is a prime place for corrosion too.

Below: A-pillars corrode where they meet the roof.

and above and below the screen on Montego saloons. The screens are bonded in place so it's best to leave repair to a professional. Maestro tailgates can rust beneath the window, but tailgate replacement is easy enough if you can source the panel.

The front valance of the Maestro van and entry level Maestro car is metal rather than plastic; it can attract stone chips which will blossom into rust unless treated. Behind the bumpers of plastic bumper cars are metal valances which weren't always fully painted at

Above: Weakness here can compromise structural integrity.

Below: The top of the rear screen is a Montego trouble spot.

The rear of the screen surround is equally prone to rust.

the factory, and any rust here can accelerate quickly. In some cases, corrosion in the boot floor is the earliest visible sign. Blisters on the door bottoms indicate trapped water which will develop into more serious corrosion if ignored.

Fuel filler pockets corrode as water can be trapped behind the slight lip caused by the wing and filler pocket joint, and fuel filler pipes can corrode through because of trapped mud in the wheel arches – especially if they're rarely cleaned out. Cars with body kits can

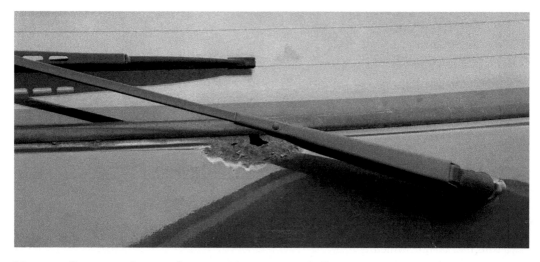

Maestro tailgates can also corrode, as can Montego estate tailgates.

Above: Blistering door bottoms usually the result of water between the skins.

Below: All four doors can suffer and can be repaired if caught quickly.

corrode under the spoilers and skirts, so check thoroughly. And for pre-1988 Montegos, check to see if they're on the original metric wheels. Tyres can be hard to source, and it's wise to fit imperial wheels from a later car.

Most examples you will find for sale today have Flint Grey interiors – the most common colour, which is good for sourcing spare plastic trim. Some colours – notably Mink and Bounty Blue – can be difficult to source, and we would recommend avoiding

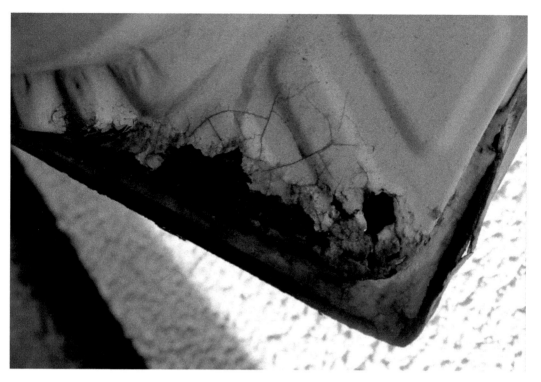

Above: Inside is usually worse the outside for door corrosion.

Below: Fuel filler pockets can corrode – this is far from the worst.

Filler necks can suffer from corrosion as mud traps water in the arches.

these unless interiors are perfect. Brown interior plastics as used with Sandpiper, Bitter Chocolate and Caramel interiors are prone to UV damage, which can leave them brittle and difficult to remove without causing damage. Model-specific items such as seats and door cards with particular fabrics and colours can be hard to source, so ensure you buy the best interior you can find. It's worth noting that L-spec cars pre-1988 used a type of tweed that is prone to water staining, so marks on the seats should come as no surprise. In many cases a wet vacuum will help. Upmarket Vanden Plas and Mayfair models had walnut trim to the door cards – check for cracked lacquer. These cars may not be expensive, but the restoration process of the wood is no different from a Rolls-Royce. Leather seats where specified on Vanden Plas and some GSi models are the easiest to repair, given the common material, but you might find yourself lucky enough to come across a trimmer with similar materials to original cloths. Early Maestro dashboards rattle, but the later one-piece unit tends to be fairly rattle free. Its problem is that it can crack and lift above the instrument binnacle. No successful repairs have been enacted for the lift at the time of publication, though cracks can be opened and filled with success. Some electrical gadgets can be suspect, notably central locking and electric windows, but these systems are simple and easily fixed.

Entry-level models used the 1.3-litre A-series, as also seen in the outgoing Allegro and Ital ranges. These engines have few major issues and spares are easily sourced owing to their fitment in the Mini. Pre-1984, the 1.6 Maestro used a short-lived engine known as the R-series, developed from the E-series and fitted with a timing chain. Early MGs used

Body kits can hide rust – check carefully.

Metric wheels for pre-1987 Montegos. Tyres are hard to source.

Brown interiors suffer UV damage; grey trim is hardier.

a Weber carburettor, Austins an SU. This continued beyond 1984 with the new S-series, more thoroughly revamped, featuring a timing belt and non-interference cylinder head, so you needn't worry about causing too much damage should the belt snap. Again, there are few issues inherent with these units. You may be worried by emulsification in the oil filler tube – this is caused by the routing of the filler pipe and is a design flaw rather than a sign of head gasket failure as in most. The 2.0 models used the O-series as seen in the Princess; carburetted for some Montegos, more commonly fitted with electronic fuel injection. This is also the engine used for the MG EFi and (with a carburettor) MG Turbo variants of both the Maestro and Montego. These can leak oil, but it's nothing to worry about as long as they're kept topped up. The final development of these engines is the renowned MDi diesel, known by many as the Perkins Prima. In naturally aspirated or turbocharged forms this is an economical and reliable unit.

There was a choice of two manual and two automatic gearboxes, depending upon the engine chosen. 1.3- and 1.6-litre Maestros, and Austin Montegos with the same engines, used a manual gearbox derived from that used in the Volkswagen Golf. Entry-level models used a four-speed variant while more plush variants gained a fifth gear. While the gearbox is reliable, the linkages are prone to disconnecting and a vague shift might indicate linkage wear. 1.6-litre models were also available with automatic transmission, a three-speed unit also sourced from Volkswagen.

2.0 models, and all Rover Montegos, used a gearbox jointly developed with Honda and first used in the Austin Montego 2.0. This gearbox, the PG1, was used in several other Rover and Honda products through to the MG ZS180 in 2005. This gearbox was also used

Good examples are hard to find, but worth preserving.

in all diesel models. Again, this box can suffer with worn linkages, though not to the same extent and these can also be repaired. Some 2.0 models were available with a four-speed ZF automatic used widely in the industry.

Neither the Maestro nor Montego is an expensive car to buy today, though the MG models attract interest, and the Turbos are significantly more valuable than other examples. The rarer and older these cars get the greater interest will become, and it is only necessary to look at the rising values of their predecessors to see the path that the Maestro and Montego will take. Perhaps these cars would not be wise as investments. But you shouldn't lose out if you're the sort of buyer who cares more about overall enjoyment of your purchase than about making money from it.